Choosing Change

Titus Naso

Tomis Press

Choosing Change
Titus Naso

Copyright ©2022 by Titus Naso. All rights reserved.

Published by Tomis Press
Silverton, Oregon

This work is an edited excerpt from a larger work, which was previously copyrighted by Titus Naso in 2021 under the title, "Annum Poetica."

Hardcover ISBN: 978-1-958337-01-1
Paperback ISBN: 978-1-958337-16-5
E-Book ISBN: 978-1-958337-17-2

Titus Naso is a pen name of Jesse S. Smith.

titusnaso.com • tomispress.com • jessesmithbooks.com

Poetry / Self-Help / Motivational

Introduction

You are here to do something amazing with your life.

You can make conscious choices that will have long-term positive impacts on your future and the futures of others.

You can choose to learn to focus your mind; and as your mindset changes, your life will change.

I wrote these poems during an intense period of personal transformation.

In the early days of the Covid-19 pandemic, during the global lockdowns in April of 2020, I challenged myself to write a poem a day for a year.

The poems presented here were forged in the fire of my own journey of personal transformation during that tumultuous year; and they have been seared onto these pages, still glowing with that heat.

In the context of a process of transformation, a few of these poems reveal deeply personal struggles. We all must struggle at times to overcome obstacles in our lives.

Thank you for sharing this journey with me. I hope that these poems will be inspiring and motivational for you, my friends.

Peace,

Titus Naso
April 2, 2022

Start Strong

Gratitude, Not Bitterness

Let gratitude, not bitterness,
  be the focus of my mind:
appreciation, thankfulness,
  and trying to be kind.

For blessings down upon me rain,
  beauty before my eyes:
when I can look around again,
  these things I realize.

So gratitude, not bitterness,
  shall all my focus be:
appreciation, thankfulness,
  recurring thoughts for me.

The Goal Achieved

I achieved a major goal today
and yet that goal's not gone away –
although I've checked it off my list,
I haven't seen the last of it!
Although this battle has been won
(and sometimes it was kind of fun)
completing it was just step one,
I'm never really truly done.
I guess that's why they call it work,
and I don't want to be a jerk
so I have to accept the fact
my goal achieved is just the first act.

A Bonfire of Memories

I made a pile of memories
    I wanted to forget,
of stress and shame and ancient pain
    and dreams not come true yet.

I piled them in a jumble,
    I piled them up quite high.
They looked a mess, I do confess,
    but still I had to try.

I set those memories on fire
    and watched them burn away.
Though my brain contains their ashen remains
    I'm free to live a new day.

The Exception

There's an exception to that rule!
Sometimes we make ourselves a fool
and tell ourselves more lies
when we tend to generalize:
"It's *never* good, it's *always* bad,
  this meal is just the *worst* I've had!"
If we don't want our lives to stink
perhaps we must change how we think.

A Dash of "What the Hell"

With a little bit of "fuck it"
    and a dash of "what the Hell"
I set my feet on a new path,
    left the one they knew so well.

With a little bit of "You got this"
    I decided to make that change,
Ignoring all the naysayers
    who said I was deranged.

Believing I could make that change
    I chose to take a new route;
And now at last I can enjoy
    my labor's well-earned fruit!

How It Started

The Creek Walk

We walked down to the creek this eve,
enjoyed a pleasant moment there.
The birds were singing in the trees
and fragrant scents perfumed the air.
The grass was wet from earlier rain,
the evening warm as day more fair.

From mess and fuss we need a break,
a quiet moment's peace to take.
We should go down there every day,
it really is not far away
and only takes a little time
and always brings such peace of mind –
tho clouds of grey mimicked my cares,
which chase me 'bout like Furies fierce
whose whips and torches give no rest,
and calm times with their shrieks do pierce!
Sadly, that's what my mind does best.

But Nature brings perspective back,
fills up with beauty what I lack.
So blessings on the trees and stream,
this life, better than any dream;
and fittingly for my dark brain,
the ev'ning now has turned to rain.

I Am

profound, foolish
lighthearted, grumpy
serene, quarrelsome
idealistic, cynical
human

Always to Seek

I would not have for inner peace to quest
if it was something I at first possessed.
I would not need for balance still to strive
if it was simply part of being alive.
But it is my nature always to seek –
that's who I am, it's not just some mystique!

Appreciation

Admiring Nature

I stand here on the banks of flowing creek
admiring flowers, butterflies, and birds
on the first day of June, early summer.
All Nature is bright, and filled with great hope
while my dog looks expectant, and wonders
why I delay when there's so much to see.

Just a Note

Just a note to you
to thank you for this life
that you have made with me,
my darling sweet wife.

Rhododendron Flowers

A-buzzing are the bees that fly about
the blossoms of the rhododendron bush,
the flowers fully opened now, fancy,
a brilliant bright color cacophony:
riotous radiant red, pretty pink,
luscious lavender, wholesome white, glowing
illuminated by bright beams of sun
to them giving a glow of godlike grace,
the huge heads of these fresh flowers us uplift.

Cottonwood Fluff

puffy white tufts
bits of fluff
drifting from the sky
but can you guess why?
you might think it's snow,
but that's not it, oh no,
for this fluff is the seeds
of the cottonwood trees!

June in Haiku

birds sing in the trees
only aware of the now
night's rain storms have passed

sun shines on the grass
the day is cheerful and bright
last night, the storm raged

the sky is cloudy
drought no longer worries us
the grass is happy

A *Pleasant Stroll*

The evening sun was so pleasant that I
went for a stroll without destination
to feel the sunbeams shine upon my face
and to enjoy the coolness of the air.
Around the corner, to the fence post's end
walked I, while serenaded by the birds.
This truly is a wondrous land of bliss.
Though weeds have grown wild-tall with all this rain,
I love how nature-close our farm life feels.

The World's Throne

Looking upwards at the sky of blue,
the wind blows through the trees of green.
Orange flowers bloom for me and you,
most beautiful we've ever seen.

The rippling current of the stream
flows on, between banks, over stones.
If everything's indeed a dream,
then wherever you sit is the world's throne.

The Rabbit

I will tell you a little of myself.
I live so far out in the countryside
that my driveway is surprisingly long.
This evening, while dragging out to the street
my trash and recycling carts down the drive,
they made so much noise, I could not listen
to my podcast; and my aching right toe
with the broken toenail was pushing up
against the edge of my boot as I walked
hauling these trash cans out to the road edge
and thinking to myself, "This life is it.
  This is the best life I could ask for.
  This is the life I have chosen to live.
  This is the best life I could ever have.
  The rest of the details are up to me.
  Whatever has not worked yet: up to me.
  Mistakes I'd rather forget: up to me.
  The sunset is coming this way; up to me
  to bring color to this day, and live free.
  Whatever details are left are my own,
  details I still have to deal with someday;
  but I am a man full-grown;
  I'll figure it all out in my way.
  There always seems to be one detail
      out of grasp –
  it's not the first time, and you've already failed
      at this task.

But the motivational speakers
    still want you to believe
everything you dream of
    you can still achieve
       if you just ask:
let success shine down from above
and in the glow of universal love
       you will bask."

I left the cans out by the road,
and began to walk home, quiet without my load.
While walking, I was thinking all these thoughts
about this strange path through life that's my lot,
when I was quite surprised to see
a rabbit in my path – coney!
A skinny one at that, scrawny,
and brown, with fluffy tail shown me.
But that was later – first, it hopped up near
to investigate me, showing no fear,
as close to me as I am now to you,
an experience of what in life is really true:
a moment, when all the Universe is born anew,
    and another
    and another
    and another
in an infinite cascade,
reflected and mirroring beyond
our comprehension, into the realm
of pure abstract imagination:
    formless
    nameless
    timeless
    bodyless
    beingness.

A Cleansing Rain
or, The Parting of the Clouds

It rained so hard today,
it washed sadness away.
The storm clouds parted, and I'm
ready for a new day.

Yesterday's Rain

The rippling water sound in the stream bed
and cheerful birds in branches overhead
the warm summer sun and the clear blue skies
yesterday's rain showers and chill breeze belies.

Moonlight Through Clouds

So thick and grey they obscure the sky
and yet there's light to see:
tho stars be hid by the clouds up high,
the moonlight's enough for me.

Choosing Change

Mud

"mud slows me down" I wrote
in my smartphone fitness tracker app's hist'ry note
reflecting, I saw, on a deeper level it's true:
for spiritual mud slows me down, too

Sad Insights

I looked at old notes from my shelf
and there within I found a wealth
of sad insights about myself,
of inner demons and mental health.

Those early writings tell the tale
of inner screaming, as I wailed –
and just as I had caught my breath
came suddenly face to face with death.

There is Always More, or Less

There is always more to say.
I could write a poem every day
on worries, and projects, piled on the floor;
but sometimes less is more.

Rise Above

Sometimes we get too down on ourselves.
We spiral where the darkness dwells;
and many pieces have to move
before things will start to improve.

But there is always hope when you look,
from other people, or a self-help book;
and in time, we can finally rise above
and begin to dwell in a place of love.

"Personality Isn't Permanent"

All of us are changing, ev'ry day;
    sometimes for better, sometimes for worse.
It shows in what we think and what we say,
    it affects the life story that we rehearse.
Now it's become a rebellious act just to suggest
    there's anything flexible about identity,
but that's a thought we must embrace to be our best:
    we really can decide who we want to be.
The haters scream out, "No! You are who you are,
    and the worst moment of your life is the real you!"
We've got to say "Fuck those guys" if we want to go far
    and let our higher aspirations shine on through.

Change

It does not occur at a constant pace:
sometimes too slow, sometimes a frantic race,
sometimes too much, more often not enough.
Although the very thought fills some with fear
there's been an awful lot of it this year
and more is coming! and it may be rough.
The world around us often seems quite strange:
rather than fear it, let us welcome change.

Revisions

How many times did John Milton revise
the opening book of *Paradise Lost*?
How many revisions did Dante write
as he composed the *Comedy Divine*?
How many changes did Homer endure,
how many Ovid, Catullus, Shakespeare?

When we read Tennyson, we only see
his finished work, we do not know how he
revised and rearranged his complex lines,
much imagery compressed in a small space –
reworking the wording and the phrases
of his intensely creative first draft.

Taking Control

Happiness from Moment to Moment

Like a child who's playing in the sand,
not caring she a futile task pursues;
or a man with fortune in his hand –
hey, at least he enjoys singin' the blues!
True happiness in life is not some distant goal:
you feel it from moment to moment in your soul.

Take a Moment

'Tis the season to live in the moment:
let go of the past, and future worries;
release anger and resentment and pain.
Allow all negativity to float
away into the clear blue summer sky,
and listen to the breeze blow through the leaves.
Feel the warmth of the sunshine on your face.
Enjoy each breath. Take a moment to be.

Just Be

I've heard a lot of advice,
some of it from people wise;
but focusing on my breath has never worked for me,
so this morning I tried the mantra, "Just be."
When I focus too much on my breath,
it gets all wonky and feels like death.
This has forced me to face the facts:
thoughts of breathing don't help me relax.
But inner peace is important to find;
I need a way to clear my mind.
By concentrating on my "Just be" mantra words,
I may be able to eliminate mental turds.

Sometimes, Forgiveness is Hard

I forgive you
I forgive you
I forgive you
It's hard
It's hard
It's hard
I forgive you
I forgive you
I forgive you

Luckier Than Most

Even when things go wrong, I'm fortunate;
even in bad times, luckier than most.
I must focus my mind on gratitude
to reflect on blessings, but not to boast.

The Cosmological Constant

Albert Einstein once second-guessed himself,
announced his equation was incorrect:
the 'cosmological constant' he'd used,
represented by Greek letter 'lambda' (Λ)
had been an error, as he now believed
based on Edwin Hubble's discoveries
of an ever-expanding universe.
But decades later, long after he'd died,
astrophysicists revived old 'lambda'
to account for the acceleration
of that same universal expansion.
Einstein, it turned out, was right the first time:
his error lay in thinking he was wrong.
Have faith in yourself. Don't ever give up:
for you, too, may someday be proven right
by poorly understood Dark Energy.

We Each Must Choose

To chance our lives we cannot leave
if we our goals wish to achieve.
A conscious path we each must choose
if we our goals wish to pursue.
Envision ourselves at the heights we'll soar
if from our lives we wish for more.
Then write we out a detailed plan,
if we wish to do the best we can.

Being My Best Self

I'm setting myself deadlines,
trying to take control of my time.
To overcome my uncertain mind,
I'm setting myself deadlines.

I'm writing out my long-term goals,
I know they will be good for my soul.
Gonna turn my mental shit into gold
by writing out my long-term goals.

I'm planning how my life will change,
tho some people might think it strange:
if I want it to rearrange,
I must plan how my life will change.

I want to learn to be my best,
it matters not who is impressed.
I do not like to be distressed,
so I must learn to be my best!

Fat Guitar Tone

Give me that fat tone, with the booming bass,
the ballsy mids fill out the punchy sound,
and just enough high end to make it shine.
Too often the sound's nothing but treble,
it sounds tinny and dull, flat and lifeless,
a deadpan transistor without a soul.
No, no more, get that shit away from me!
I'm switching my guitar to heavier strings,
a tube amp for a warm distortion sound,
and overdrive pedals for my high gain!

Judgments

Never Cease

"No one believes in me, 'cause I have failed!"
the old man moaned, he sniffled, and he wailed.
"No matter if I in myself believe,
  the world shall ne'er offer me a reprieve:
  for people love to judge and to condemn;
  and once they start, there's no escaping them.
  If I should someday meet with some success,
  they'd chase me down to tell me I'm a mess!
  It's too late now, I cannot over start,
  so I must find acceptance in my heart."
Then started he again, heaving a sigh.
Despite it all, he'd never cease to try.

Leaping to Judgment
Inspired by Dante, *Paradiso*, Canto XIII lines 112-140

Thy feet thou shouldst move slowly
    like as though they were filled with lead
rather than leap to judgments
    and let assumptions fill thy head.

Too often we most thoughtlessly
    do cry out "Yes!" or "No!"
but when we fail to give matters thought
    we are brought down quite low.

When we quickly to judgment leap,
    often false is our choice.
Then, rather than admit we've made a mistake
    we'll defend it with our last voice.

For we're too full of confidence
    when arrogant vanity assumes –
the intellect admits no wrong,
    such errors lead to doom!

Shouldst thou go seeking for the truth
    yet not apply rational thought,
then thou art like to ne'er return –
    so recall what you were taught.

Think of the brambles in winter-time
    that look like dry dead vines
yet burst forth into floral blooms
    when on them summer sun shines.

Reck not the harvest afore it's ripe
    nor chickens before they hatch,
and guess not which of thy neighbors sins most:
    for there are limits to thy watch!

The Fruit Seller's Tale

A tale is told on dark evenings
    about a man with a fruit stall
who performed an experiment
    on his customers, one and all.

He took two identical bunches of grapes
    and sold them side by side.
He put different labels upon each bin –
    but both of those labels lied!

For one of those bins was labeled "Us"
    and "Them" the other label read;
and the bin labeled "Us," it sold out fast,
    while the other was left for dead.

The name it mattered not at all,
    for the grapes were just the same:
some were juicy, and some were flawed;
    yet people chose based on the name.

So the Keeper tried again, as a trial now and then:
    when the *same fruit* was labeled "Good" or "Bad,"
then everyone complained about the "Bad" –
    but they said "Good" was the best they'd had!

Yet another effect the shopkeeper noticed
    as he tried this again, over time:
because no one ever bought the grapes labeled "Bad,"
    those ones rotted on the vine.

Yes, the label predicted the outcome,
    for it told the people what to do.
Because they believed what the label said,
    eventually they made the name come true!

Labels Ain't My Bag

Take that label off me,
    I don't want a tag!
I just want to be free –
    labels ain't my bag.

Sometimes we mock the other side
    for being "sensitive,"
accusing them of tryin' to hide –
    but *we* have no fucks to give...

Until they treat us the same way:
    we find the tables turned;
we wish they would watch what they say,
    for now we feel quite burned!

Too often we label sisters and brothers
    and we think it is just fine;
but then when we are labeled by others
    they tell us, "Don't you whine!"

As long as we identify
    them with labels we choose
we never are inclined to try
    to challenge words we use.

It's only when we find we've been
    labeled by enemies,
we tend to reprimand them then –
    "No, don't talk like that, please!"

Yes, sticks and stones may break my bones
    but words may hurt me worse;
for wounds heal when I'm left alone,
    but confidence destroyed is hard to reverse.

Vibrations

We know not how others our words affect
as each of us is struggling through our days
obsessing over what's true and correct.
Vibrations ripple out in many ways
from each and every message that we send
as we with others do communicate;
what they hear's not always what we intend,
so patience and love we must demonstrate.
I was inspired, and perhaps I was scared,
by a story a friend recently confessed
about how the mind really will "go there"
when a person is sufficiently distressed.
But a simple word of encouragement well-timed
can be enough to change another's frame of mind.

Though calling out public bad behavior
was not in fact my initial intent
when I sat down to write, on this day here:
still, down the rabbit hole my dark thoughts went.
I soon began of bad habits to speak
whereby we people spread feelings of hate
by calling others "narcissist" or "freak" –
putting others down makes nobody great.
With words of condemnation and judgment,
some find that hurting others is their power.
We must ask ourselves, "Is that what I meant?
 And is it worth dwelling on these thoughts sour?"
Even my poem from its intended topic strayed:
through habit and complacency, mistakes are made.

The Whispering of the Shades

Inspired by Dante's *Purgatorio*, Book I.115-130 and Book V.10-21

My Guide indicated the dewy grass
whereon I stretched myself with grateful tears
as he cleansed me of that all-cov'ring grime
that had clung to me as I traversed Hell.

"Why allow your mind to be fixated
  to the point that you lose momentum?"
my Guide asked me crossly. "Why does it matter
  to you what these Shades whisper here? Come on.
  Always, people will talk. You must let them.
  A man who becomes mired in his own thoughts
  loses sight of goals. Worry blunts purpose.
  Stand as tall and sturdy as a mountain,
  whose peak sways not in the mightiest wind."

Part of a Team

It's lonely to stand alone 'gainst the world
with every man's hand always against you
    like Ishmael.
It brings hope to hear words of agreement,
support, or even a cherished friendship:
    part of a team.

Each One

Each one of us has seen
    through years what we have seen.
That's why we each believe
    what each of us believes.
And through our lives we try
    to do what seems to us right.
The past shapes our sense of self
    and the values for which we fight.

The Same

All humans are just people
 no matter what folks claim.
We talk about "good" and "evil"
 but we're really all the same.

A Word to the Wise

Ampelos

Precaution we must all be sure to take
when out upon a branch we clamber far,
for easy 'tis to make a bad mistake,
then to the ground we tumble, and fall hard –
just like Ampelos, youth of lovely locks.
A juicy grape his arm stretched forth to pluck
'til suddenly he slipped and tumbled off
the branch, and to his death fell, screaming "Fuck!"
God Bacchus libertine had loved him well
and heard the scream echo from hills afar
as from the elm tree bright Ampelos fell;
so grieving Bacchus placed him in the stars.
Now even when Arcas from the sky sets,
Ampelos shines so we will not forget.

Another Task

I gave myself another task,
I thought it not too much to ask;
for it'd take but a little while...
And so I put it on the pile
of all my tasks not done before,
and tossed them all into a drawer.

I Must Remember

Perhaps I must remember to ask
before beginning a new task,
"Is this really something I have time to do?" –
and force myself to answer true.

O Heart, Beware

The Springtime's fair
fresh is the air
O heart, beware
of too much care.

A Mind On Fire

A good fire under control may provide
a source of heat to warm the house, cook food,
fire a forge, or run a diesel engine.
But when a fire in the back of one's mind
is unconstrained in its intensity,
it burns all it touches, leaves only ash,
and provides no benefits: only pain.

Between Extremes

"The summer is too hot,
the winter is too cold.
First you are too young,
and then you are too old."

When nothing will suffice,
perhaps it would be nice,
rather than wish away,
to just enjoy today.

How It's Going

75 Hard Begins

Perhaps it seems a strange thing for a bard –
today I begin "75 Hard,"
a mental toughness and fitness program.
I'm hopeful this will help change who I am:
a structured routine my life to revamp,
myself through paces put, like a boot camp!

I plan my life to change in many ways,
jump-start with the next 75 days.
And when I reach the end, I'll give a shout:
thus my poetic year I shall close out.

The Power of Affirmation

An affirmation power has, I'm told,
our attitudes and thoughts to shape and guide.
Could this help me to combat patterns old,
and negativity I keep inside?
Perhaps 'twill help me to gain some control
over perpetual darkling spiral down –
envisioning fulfillment of a goal
could really help to turn one's life around.
I'm told to state it in the present tense
and squelch that nagging voice that screams out, "Lie!"
Believing things could happen makes some sense;
embodying my goals is worth a try.
Affirming vision's hope, perhaps I'll find
that confidence is just a state of mind.

A Visualization

I am a writer, and I've always been.
I am a musician, since way back when.
I've been an entrepreneur now for decades.
People love my work, it wins accolades.
My books are read by people I don't know.
My songs are playing on the radio.
And for my business work, folks give me thanks!
I have a fortune saved up in the bank.
I had to hire a slew of employees
to keep up with new customers saying, "Please!"
I have paid off all of my family's debts.
I've made an impact folks will ne'er forget.

My Internal Judge Criticizes My Visualization

I write these words while sitting on the couch,
so far from them, my brain is screaming, "Ouch!"
Perhaps if these goals I can make myself say,
these affirmations of mine will be true someday.

75 Hard Continues

My Lent ritual I early began.
Among other men, I am just a man.
Although perhaps uncommon for a bard,
I persevere at "75 Hard"
despite the power outages and ice,
I have not given in – though it'd be nice!
    I'm sticking with the program
    and changing who I am:
no alcohol; and two workouts a day,
each 45 minutes, and one outside.
Just a couple more things before I play,
just a couple more things before I ride:
a daily shirtless selfie, please don't shriek;
a gallon of water (gotta take a leak);
    pick a diet and stick to it,
    that's the only way to do it;
and read ten pages of a self-help book,
changing how I think, not just how I look.

Life's Strange Looking-Glass

Although on projects I'm falling behind,
at least I don't feel I'm losing my mind.
I surely have felt that way in the past,
such as last summer; but it did not last.
The lightning storm has cleared up in my head;
on other things I can focus instead.
It's true, sometimes I still have thoughts I hate,
but I'm less likely to persevorate.
I don't think this was due to any trick:
when neurons misfire, my brain is a dick!
It took some time and calm for it to pass.
Now I reflect on life's strange looking-glass,
consider what future will make me glad
as husband, writer, musician, and Dad.

75 Days Later

Can you believe it's been seventy-five
long days since I began the challenge hard?
I am so fortunate to be alive,
regardless of my talents as a bard.
I can report that I'm both pleased and shocked,
for me, this was quite a tremendous win:
full twenty-two pounds in this time I have dropped –
it's been two decades since I was this thin!

By social media haters called deranged,
by toxic friends from my past written off.
I made a choice, and my life I have changed!
Yes, now it's on, no matter how they scoff.
And I will never stop until I've won:
with this round over, my fight's just begun!

An Auspicious Conclusion

Blue are the skies, the sunny Springtime skies,
without a cloud, no, not one hint of rain.
I have been reading Ovid's *Fasti* poems,
and poet's inspiration I pursued.
Today is quite auspicious to complete
this book of poetry, and I thank you
dear reader, you have joined in this journey.

Now go in peace, dear reader, spread the love,
teach one another to be tolerant;
but for injustice, give no quarter, none –
not even when it comes from your own side!
Remember always, please, that life can change:
our personality and circumstance.
No matter if you're stuck, or in exile,
you can contentment find, there's always hope;
never forget that there is always hope.

*Go forth
and
Be awesome*

References and Resources

The "75 Hard" Mental Toughness Program was created and promoted by Andy Frisella. You can learn more about the program from the following links:

Overview: "75 Hard | The 75-Day Tactical Guide to Winning the War with Yourself"
https://andyfrisella.com/pages/75hard-info

Podcast: "75HARD: A 75-Day Tactical Guide to Winning the War With Yourself, with Andy Frisella - MFCEO290"
https://andyfrisella.com/blogs/mfceo-project-podcast/75hard-a-75-day-tactical-guide-to-winning-the-war-with-yourself-with-andy-frisella-mfceo291

Book: "75 Hard: A Tactical Guide to Winning the War with Yourself" by Andy Frisella.
https://andyfrisella.com/products/75-hard-a-tactical-guide-to-winning-the-war-with-yourself

I referenced a number of Wikipedia entries through the year. I have not cited all of these articles individually, but I thank Wikipedia as an invaluable resource to the layperson who wishes to pursue a variety of interests.

I additionally consulted a number of reference materials and resources:

Abrams, M.H., et al., editors. (1993 ed.) *The Norton Anthology of English Literature: Sixth Edition, Volume 1.* New York, NY: W. W. Norton & Company

Alighieri, Dante. (1952 ed.). *The Divine Comedy of Dante Alighieri: Translated by Charles Eliot Norton.* Great Books of the Western World vol. 21: Dante. Chicago, IL: The University of Chicago Press (Encyclopædia Britannica, Inc.)

Alighieri, Dante. (2006 ed). *Paradise from the Divine Comedy: read by Heathcote Williams.* Audiobook. Naxos AudioBooks via Libby.

Alighieri, Dante. (2006 ed.) *Purgatory from the Divine Comedy: read by Heathcote Williams.* Audiobook. Naxos AudioBooks via Libby.

Amen, Daniel G. (2008 ed.) *Change Your Brain, Change Your Life.* Narrated by the author. Audiobook. Random House Audio via Libby.

Angelou, Maya. (2006). *Celebrations: Rituals of Peace and Prayer, Read by the Author. An Unabridged Production.* Audiobook. Random House Audio via Libby.

Angus, David. (2006 ed.). *Moses.* Audiobook. Read by Kerry Shale. Audiobook. Naxos Audiobooks via Libby.

Aurelius, Marcus (Maxwell Staniforth, trans. & introd.) (1964 ed.) *Meditations.* New York, NY: Penguin Books USA Inc. (Penguin Classics).

Bede. (trans, ed, intro, notes & commentary by Faith Wallis). (2012 ed). *Bede: The Reckoning of Time, Translated with introduction, notes and commentary by Faith Wallis.* Translated Texts for Historians, Volume 29. Liverpool, UK: Liverpool University Press. [I have tremendous respect for Professor Wallis, she has done amazing work with very thorough scholarship.]

Ben-Shahar, Tal. (2007). *Happier: Learn the Secrets to Daily Joy and Lasting Fulfillment.* San Francisco, CA: McGraw-Hill.

Blake, William. (David V. Erdman, ed., Harold Bloom, notes). (1988 ed.). *The Complete Poetry and Prose of William Blake: Newly Revised Edition.* New York, NY: Anchor Books (Random House, Inc.)

Blake, William. (2005 ed.). *William Blake: Selected Poems.* Read by Frederick Davidson. Audiobook. Blackstone Audio, Inc. and Buck 50 Productions, LLC via Libby.

Brown, Brené. (2015 ed.) *Rising Strong: How the Ability to Reset Transforms the Way We Live, Love, Parent, and Lead. Read by the Author | Unabridged.* Audiobook. Random House Audio via Libby.

Catullus. (trans. Guy Lee). (1998 ed.) *The Poems of Catullus: Edited and translated with an Introduction and Notes by Guy Lee.* Oxford, UK: Oxford University Press (Oxford World's Classics).

Chaucer, Geoffrey. (trans. David Wright). (1988 ed.) *The Canterbury Tales: A verse translation with an Introduction and Notes by David Wright.* Aylesbury, Bucks: Oxford University Press (The World's Classics).

Chaucer, Geoffrey. (2005 ed). *The Canterbury Tales: Volume II.* Read by Philip Madoc, Frances Jeater, John Rowe, Charles Simpson and John Moffatt. Naxos AudioBooks via Libby.

Chaucer, Geoffrey. (1952 ed.) *Troilus and Cressida and The Canterbury Tales by Geoffrey Chaucer: with modern English versions of both works.* Great Books of the Western World vol. 22: Chaucer. Chicago, IL: The University of Chicago Press (Encyclopædia Britannica, Inc.)

Cohen, Marshall. (July 9, 2020). *'Broken heart syndrome' has increased during the Covid-19 pandemic, small study suggests.* CNN. https://www.cnn.com/2020/07/09/health/broken-heart-syndrome-coronavirus-wellness/index.html

Dickinson, Emily. (Christanne Miller, ed.). (2016). *Emily Dickinson's Poems As She Preserved Them.* Cambridge, MA: The Belknap Press of Harvard University Press.

Dodge, Theodore Ayrault. (orig. 1889, 2005 ed.) *Hannibal: Introduction by Ian M. Cuthbertson.* New York, NY: Barnes & Noble, Inc.

Doyle, Arthur Conan. (2009 ed.). *The Adventures of Sherlock Holmes.* Narrated by Ralph Cosham. Audiobook. Blackstone Publishing via Libby.

Eratosthenes and Hyginus. (Robin Hard, trans., introd. & notes). (2015). *Constellation Myths with Aratus's Phaenomena.* Oxford, UK: Oxford University Press (Oxford World's Classics).

Epicurus (George K. Strodach, trans. & introd., foreword by Daniel Klein). (2012 ed.) *The Art of Happiness.* New York, NY: Penguin Books (Penguin Group USA, Inc.)

Frankl, Victor E. (2004 ed.) *Man's Search for Meaning.* Narrated by Simon Vance. Audiobook. Blackstone Audio, Inc. and Buck 50 Productions, LLC via Libby.

Frost, Robert. (1969 ed.) *The Poetry of Robert Frost: Edited by Edward Connery Lathem.* New York: Holt, Rinehart and Winston.

Goggins, David. (2018). *Can't Hurt Me: Master Your Mind and Defy the Odds.* (Sorry, APA format, but no location is printed anywhere on the book.) Lioncrest Publishing.

Hanson, Rick and Mendius, Richard. (2011). *Meditations to Change Your Brain.* Audiobook. Sounds True via Libby.

Hardy, Benjamin P. (2016). *How to Consciously Design Your Ideal Future.* Brooklyn, NY: Thought Catalog Books.

Hardy, Benjamin. (2020). *Personality Isn't Permanent: Break Free from Self-Limiting Beliefs and Rewrite Your Story.* New York, NY: Portfolio / Penguin (Penguin Random House LLC).

Harper, Faith G. (2018 ed.) *Unf*ck Your Brain: Using Science to Get Over Anxiety, Depression, Anger, Freak-Outs, and Triggers.* Read by the author. Audiobook. Blackstone Publishing via Libby.

Harris, Dan and Warren, Jeffrey with Adler, Carlye. (2017 ed.) *Meditation for Fidgety Skeptics. Read by Dan Harris and Jeff Warren. Unabridged.* Audiobook. Random House Audio via Libby.

Heath, Chip and Heath, Dan. (2010 ed.) *Switch: How to Change Things When Change Is Hard.* Narrated by Charles Kahlenberg. Audiobook. Random House Audio via Libby.

Irving, Washington. (ed & intro Austin McC. Fox). (1962 ed). *The Legend of Sleepy Hollow and other selections from Washington Irving: Edited and with an Introduction by Austin McC. Fox.* New York, NY: Washington Square Press (Pocket Books New York, a division of Simon & Schuster, Inc.)

Keats, John. (2007 ed.). *John Keats: Poems.* Read by Douglas Hodge. Audiobook. HighBridge Audio via Libby.

Keats, John. (2005 ed.) *Realms of Gold.* Narrated by Matthew Marsh and Samuel West. Audiobook. Naxos Audiobooks via Libby.

Kirton, Sarah. (n.d., c. 2002) *Primstav – an ancient calendar form – The Fall Months.* Retrieved from https://norcalspelmanslag.org/ncsnlf2002/ncsnlf2002b.html

Kross, Ethan. (2021). *Chatter: The Voice in Our Head, Why It Matters, and How to Harness It.* New York, NY: Crown (Penguin Random House LLC).

Lucretius. (Ronald Melville, trans.). (2008 ed.). *On the Nature of the Universe: A verse translation by Ronald Melville, with an Introduction and Notes by Don and Peta Fowler.* Oxford, UK: Oxford University Press (Oxford World's Classics).

Macphail, Cameron. (December 21, 2020). "Winter Solstice 2020: Why do Pagans celebrate the shortest day of the year?" *The Telegraph.* Retrieved from https://www.telegraph.co.uk/christmas/2020/12/21/winter-solstice-2020-december-shortest-day-year-what-means/

Maudslay, Francesca (director). (2010). *When Rome Ruled: War Machine*. National Geographic Television, DVD. Universal City, CA: Vivendi Entertainment (Distributor).

Milton, John. (John Leonard, ed. & introd.). (2003 ed.) *Paradise Lost*. New York, NY: Penguin Books.

Ovid. (trans, ed, intro & notes Peter Green). (2005 ed.). *The Poems of Exile: Tristia and the Black Sea Letters, With a New Foreword; Translated with an Introduction, Notes, and Glossary by Peter Green*. Berkeley, CA: University of California Press.

Ovid. (Anne & Peter Wiseman, trans, ed, & notes). (2013 ed.). *Fasti*. Oxford, UK: Oxford University Press (Oxford World's Classics).

Ovid. (trans. A.D. Melville, intro & notes E.J. Kenney; translation of "The Art of Love" by B. P. Moore with revisions by A.D. Melville). (2008 ed.) *The Love Poems*. Oxford, UK: Oxford University Press (Oxford World's Classics). [This rhyming verse translation includes all of Ovid's famous transgressive works of "love" poetry, for which he was later exiled: *Amores, Cosmetics for Ladies, Ars Amatoria,* and *Remedia Amatoria*.]

Pariser, Michael. (Foreword by Robert Glover). (2020). *No More Mr. Nice Guy: The Hero's Journey: A Step-by-Step Guide to Becoming an Integrated Male*. Published by Michael Pariser, Psy.D / Michael Pariser Psychotherapy, PC via Amazon & printed in Middletown, DE.

Smith, Jesse S. (2008 ed.). *Principles for a Self-Directed Society*. Portland, OR: Basementia Publications.

Smith, Jesse S. (2016 ed.). *Rise of the Pagans*. Silverton, Oregon: Basementia Publications.

Shakespeare, William. (2005 ed.) *The Sonnets: Read by Alex Jennings*. Audiobook. Naxos AudioBooks via Libby.

Sincero, Jen. (2017 ed.) *You Are a Badass at Making Money*. Read by Jen Sincero. Penguin Random House Audio Publishing Group: Penguin Audio via Libby.

Stillman, Janice (editor). (2020). *The Old Farmer's Almanac: 2021.* The Old Farmer's Almanac, No. 229. Dublin, OH: Yankee Publishing, Inc. [Supplied dates of astronomical and historical events.]

Sturluson, Snorri (author); Byock, Jesse L. (translation & introduction). (2005 ed.) *The Prose Edda.* New York, NY: Penguin Classics (Penguin Group (USA) Inc.).

Sun Tzu. (John Minford, trans.; Lorna Raver, introd.) (2004 ed). *The Art of War.* Narrated by Ray Porter and Lorna Raver. Audiobook. Blackstone Audio, Inc. and Buck 50 Productions, LLC via Libby.

Tennyson, Alfred. (Karen Hodder, introd. & notes). (2008 ed.) *The Works of Alfred Lord Tennyson.* Ware, Hertforshire, UK: Wordsworth Poetry Library (Wordsworth Editions Ltd.)

Thich Nhat Hanh. (2015 ed.) *Peace is Every Step: The Path of Mindfulness in Everyday Life. Foreword by H. H. the Dalai Lama. Read by Edoardo Ballerini. Edited by Arnold Kotler.* Audiobook. Blackstone Audio, Inc. and Buck 50 Productions, LLC via Libby.

Thomas, Dylan. (2006 ed.). *The Essential Dylan Thomas.* Performed by Richard Burton et al. Audiobook. Naxos Audiobooks via Libby.

Tolle, Eckhart. (2005 ed.). *Practicing the Power of Now: Essential Teachings, Meditations, and Exercises from The Power of Now.* Audiobook. New World Library via Libby.

Tyson, Neil de Grasse. (2017). *Astrophysics for People in a Hurry: Read by the Author | Unabridged.* Audiobook. Blackstone Publishing via Libby.

(unknown, trans. Benedict Flynn). (2008 ed.) *Sir Gawain and the Green Knight: New verse translation by Benedict Flynn.* Read by Jasper Britton. Naxos AudioBooks via Libby.

Various/unknown. (trans. Division of Christian Education of the National Council of the Churches of Christ in the United States of America). (1959 ed.). *The Holy Bible: Revised Standard Version* containing the Old and New Testaments, Translated from the Original Tongues. Camden, NJ: Thomas Nelson Inc.

Various / unknown. (Valerie J. Roebuck, trans. & ed.). (2010 ed.) *The Dhammapada*. New York, NY: Penguin Books (Penguin Classics & a variety of related business names).

Various. (2005 ed.). *Great Narrative Poems of the Romantic Age. (John Keats, Alfred Tennyson, William Wordsworth, Samuel Taylor Coleridge, William Morris, George Crabbe).* Narrated by John Moffatt, Samuel West, and Sarah Woodward. Audiobook. Naxos Audiobooks via Libby.

Zoll, Kenneth J. (2008). *Sinagua Sunwatchers: An Archaeoastronomy Survey of the Sacred Mountain Basin*. Sedona, AZ: Sunwatcher Publishing.